Tigers

A Carolrhoda Nature Watch Book

written and photographed by Lynn M. Stone

Carolrhoda Books, Inc. / Minneapolis

CONTENTS

For Brittany, who loves cats of all stripes, and for Cyndi and Craig, who brought me closer to tigers than I had ever been before.

Carolrhoda Books, Inc
A division of Lerner Publishing Group
241 First Avenue North
Minneapolis, MN 55401, U.S.A.

Website address: www.lernerbooks.com

Library of Congress Cataloging-in-Publication Data

Stone, Lynn M.
   Tigers / by Lynn M. Stone.
     p.   cm.
   "A Carolrhoda nature watch book."
   Includes index
   Contents: Tigers are cats — Tiger country — Born to kill — Becoming a tiger — Tracking tigers — Saving the perfect predator.
   ISBN 1-57505-578-3 (lib. bdg. : alk. paper)
   1. Tigers—Juvenile literature. [1. Tigers.] I. Title.
QL737.C23S782 2005
599.756—dc22   2003023230

Manufactured in the United States of America
1 2 3 4 5 6 – JR – 10 09 08 07 06 05

Tigers are both beautiful and dangerous.

Few humans would want to face the fury of a snarling tiger up close.

TIGERS ARE CATS

The tiger, in a single, handsome package, is everything we love—and fear—about wild animals. A tiger can be the picture of motherhood, beauty, grace, and playfulness. **Fangs** bared, lips curled, it can also be the picture of menace and snarling fury.

Perhaps no animal has a more powerful impact on human feelings than the tiger. No one looks at a tiger without feeling something. It may be a feeling of awe, joy, or sheer terror. It's one thing to admire the beauty and athletic movements of a tiger in a zoo, where we and the tiger are safe from one another. But it's another thing to stand face to **muzzle** with a tiger on a jungle trail.

The tiger is a member of the cat family and can be as playful as a house cat.

This animal that inspires so much feeling in the human spirit is one of 37 species of wild cats and one of the five "big cats," known to scientists as **Panthera,** or roaring cats. This group also includes the lion, leopard, jaguar, and snow leopard. The cougar, a wild cat of the Americas, is clearly a large cat. But the cougar does not qualify for the big cat club. What sets the *Panthera* group apart goes beyond body bulk. Members of the *Panthera* group have a special bone in their throat that allows them to roar loudly. The cougar may growl, snarl, or purr, but it cannot rumble up a throaty roar.

Except for its world-class size and roar, a tiger is in many ways very much like other cats, including house cats. A tiger has the typically short, blunt cat muzzle. It has a cat's long, sharp **canine teeth**. It has a long, narrow, agile cat body with powerful shoulders and sharp, curved claws that **retract,** or pull back, into its front paws. Like any house cat, a tiger grooms itself with a rough tongue. It spends much of its time at rest, or catnapping. And like a house cat, a sleepy tiger can suddenly change into a stealthy, stalking cat.

For many years, scientists recognized eight tiger varieties, or **subspecies:** Siberian, Bengal (Indian), Sumatran, South China, Indochinese, Caspian, Balinese, and Javan. The Caspian, Balinese, and Javan subspecies are **extinct,** or gone forever.

Tigers from the cold Russian Far East, known as Siberian or Amur tigers, tend to have lighter fur color and somewhat heavier bodies than tigers in southern Asia. Big male Siberians can be three times as heavy as male Sumatran tigers, which live on Sumatra, an island of Indonesia. A male Siberian tiger may weigh 650 pounds (295 kg). Male Sumatran tigers rarely top 250 pounds (110 kg). Tigers from the islands of Southeast Asia, such as Sumatra, have more stripes than mainland tigers.

The Sumatran tiger lives on the island of Sumatra in the Indian Ocean.

White tigers are rare in the wild. This white Siberian tiger cub was bred for his color.

White tigers are not a separate species or subspecies. They are tigers without a tiger's normal coloring. They are extremely rare in the wild. Only about a dozen wild white tigers have been seen or caught in the last 100 years, all of them in India.

White tigers are well known because they are shown in many zoos and wild animal acts. Zoos and animal breeders have bred white tigers for profit, not for the conservation, or protection, of these animals or even for educational purposes. A white tiger cub may fetch $60,000 for its owner. But to keep an assembly line of white tigers, breeders have had to mate closely related adult white tigers. The mating of closely related animals has led to the birth of many unhealthy and deformed tiger cubs. Blue-eyed white tigers fascinate crowds, but they do little to further the conservation of healthy tigers in the wild or in captivity.

The grouping of tigers into subspecies has been based largely on the somewhat different appearance of tigers from different corners of Asia. With modern laboratory techniques that account for blood factors, rather than only where tigers live and how they look, scientists are rethinking how many kinds of tigers there are. Some scientists, for example, believe that all living mainland tigers (Siberian, Bengal, South China, and Indochinese) belong to one subspecies, not four different ones. Scientists do agree that tigers on Sumatra are a separate subspecies and may even be a separate species. But whatever labels we apply to them, all tigers behave in much the same ways, whether they live in an icy, moderate, or tropical environment. Tigers are, in fact, basically the same: exceptionally large cats with an appetite for large, hoofed animals, such as deer, wild pigs, and antelope, and the skills to catch them. Where a tiger's prey lives determines to a large degree where tiger country is.

Left: *The Indochinese tiger lives in Thailand, Cambodia, and other nearby countries.* Facing page: *Like this Siberian, all tigers are very large cats that hunt other animals for food.*

TIGER COUNTRY

Tigers apparently evolved in some of the colder parts of Asia. Over time, they spread into warmer parts of Asia as well. And although tigers have disappeared from much of their former living space, they still live in an amazingly wide variety of **habitats.** Tigers of the frigid Russian Far East survive temperatures that dip to –30°F (–34°C). Yet tigers in northern India live in steamy daytime temperatures that reach 118°F (48°C).

A tiger's heavy coat helps keep it warm in cold climates. But in warm climates, tigers must cool off. They seek jungle shade on the warmest days, and they also swim and rest in streams and ponds.

Tigers live in dry forests that accumulate just 24 inches (61 cm) of rainfall yearly and in dripping tropical rain forests with 395 inches (1,000 cm) of annual rainfall. Tigers also live on grasslands, in swamps, and on sprawling plantations of oil palm, rubber, sugarcane, and coffee. Tiger habitats vary in altitude from land at sea level to mountains nearly 10,000 feet (3,000 m) high. In the eastern part of the Himalayan Mountains, tigers have been known to travel mountain passes 13,000 feet (4,000 m) above sea level.

Facing page: *Siberian tigers live in areas where the temperature may fall to –30°F (–34°C).*
Left: *Bengal tigers, which live in the steamy jungles of India, cool off in streams and ponds.*

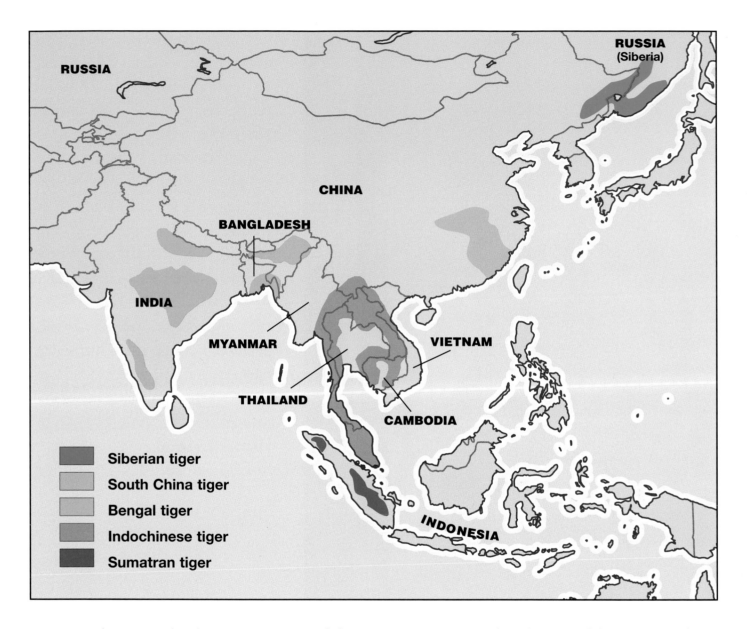

RUSSIA

RUSSIA
(Siberia)

CHINA

BANGLADESH

INDIA

MYANMAR

VIETNAM

THAILAND

CAMBODIA

INDONESIA

- Siberian tiger
- South China tiger
- Bengal tiger
- Indochinese tiger
- Sumatran tiger

Tigers live in only about 1 percent of the territory they once inhabited. They once lived in about 30 Asian countries, but they are gone from at least 15 countries, including Turkey, Iran, and Afghanistan. And in the countries that still have tigers, most live in no more than 5 percent of the land.

In countries that have wild tigers, such as China, Russia, Bangladesh, Myanmar, Cambodia, Vietnam, Thailand, and Indonesia, most have only between 100 and 500 tigers left. India, with approximately 3,000 wild tigers, is probably the only nation with more than 500.

Counting tigers is not, of course, like counting fingers and toes. Estimates of tiger populations are little more than educated guesses. Tigers are extremely difficult to count. They tend to live secretive lives and travel over broad stretches of rough, wild country.

Each adult tiger stakes out a **home range,** what we might think of as a huge estate. Unlike their African lion cousins, which live in groups called **prides,** each adult tiger lives alone and likes plenty of space for itself. Scientists have studied tigers living on home ranges as small as 7 square miles (18 sq. km) and as large as 405 square miles (1,050 sq. km). In areas where tiger **prey** is plentiful, a tiger may have a fairly small home range. Otherwise, the animal must patrol a bigger range to find enough food.

Male tigers do not have **cubs,** young tigers, at their heels, so males generally travel more widely than females and have larger home ranges. Some tiger ranges overlap. A study of tigers in Nepal showed that male tigers had from two to seven female tigers living within at least part of their home ranges. A male tiger's range, however, is less likely to overlap the ranges of other males.

Tigers hunt by themselves in their home range, a large area of land that they protect from other tigers.

Tigers will fight, if they have to, to protect their home range.

When a tiger chooses to defend its territory against another tiger, a fight may erupt. Fighting between tigers can be a bloody business. If serious fights took place often, tigers would disappear completely. But they avoid most conflicts by letting other tigers know they're around. By being forewarned, each animal can go its separate way and keep out of another tiger's space. For an adult tiger, going its separate way is most often the way it lives.

Tigers avoid many meetings by leaving messages for each other. A tiger message may just be urine or dung on the ground, or it may be the lingering scent of urine sprayed onto bushes, trees, and other objects.

In addition, tigers have **scent glands** on many parts of their bodies. By prowling along a trail, a tiger leaves scent from its toes. It can also leave scent by rubbing its cheeks on a log or rock. A tiger leaves visual messages too: scratch marks on tree trunks, flattened grass, and scrape marks made by its hind feet.

Scientists believe that one tiger probably learns a great deal from the scent and other signs left by another. The tiger that finds the scent certainly knows it is in another tiger's home range—or that a new tiger is on its home range. The strength of the scent probably reveals how recently the tiger passed, its gender, and whether it is looking for a mate. How much more the signs may tell, only the tigers know.

The tiger's voice is another tool for communication. A tiger roar can boom over 3 miles (5 km). It can signal a warning to other tigers. It can also help a **tigress** stay in touch with her cubs or help an adult tiger of either gender find a mate.

At close range, tigers "speak" with body language as well as with their growls, snarls, and moans. To show anger, for example, a tiger may stare through narrowed eyes, curl its lips, and flatten its ears.

Signs left by one tiger tell other tigers that they are entering its home range. A Siberian leaves scratch marks on a tree.

19

Prey animals usually feed at dusk or dawn, so tigers have eyes that are able to see in near darkness.

BORN TO KILL

Like all wild cats, a tiger is a **carnivore.** It lives solely on meat that it hunts and eats. And nature has given the tiger extraordinary ways—what scientists call **adaptations**—to be a successful hunter.

The tiger's keen eyesight is one such adaptation. A tiger depends largely on its eyes to find prey. A tiger sees well in daylight, but it also has sensitive vision in near darkness. Tigers usually hunt at night or in the weak light of dusk and dawn, when most prey animals are feeding and therefore on the move. A tiger probably cannot see colors or detail well, but its eyes easily detect movement, even in low light. Tigers hear well too. A tiger's hearing is probably 5 to 10 times keener than a human's. This is another adaptation to finding prey—and avoiding danger—in near darkness.

Tigers, like most cats, depend on stealth. The pads on a tiger's feet muffle sound. In poor light, a tiger's whiskers, which are sensitive to what they touch, can help warn the tiger about objects in its way.

A tiger's stripes are another adaptation for stealthy hunting. Stripes help break up the cat's outline. They camouflage the tiger by helping it blend into its surroundings.

A tiger needs to safely kill prey that may be larger than it is. The longer a large prey animal struggles, the greater the chance that it may injure its attacker, so a tiger's body is adapted to making kills swiftly and surely. A tiger's body is packed with strength. Its upper body is marvelously **limber** too. It twists and turns. The tiger's backbone is also quite flexible, which helps the cat accelerate into a 30-foot (9-m) leap or a quick burst of speed.

No adaptation for the tiger's lifestyle is more important than its canine teeth. The upper two canine teeth can be up to 2.5 inches (6.4 cm) long. The lower two can be up to 2 inches (5 cm) long. With its massive lower jaw muscles, the tiger can plunge its canines into the throat of its prey with a killing bite.

Right top: *Sensitive whiskers help a tiger find its way when there is little light.*
Right bottom: *A tiger's four canine teeth and strong jaw muscles give it a killing bite.*

A hunting tiger searches for prey, listens, lies still, and searches again. A tiger may find prey nearby, within a mile or two of where its hunt began, or it may prowl for hours over many miles looking for a meal. It often follows animal trails and even old roads. It may travel to forest clearings, swamp edges, and the water holes its prey visits. Occasionally a tiger hunts by **ambush,** waiting for prey to pass near its hiding place.

Almost any creature that crosses its path, from termite to a wild boar, can be a meal—or a snack—for a tiger. Tigers generally kill animals that weigh no more than 100 pounds (45 kg). They have been known, however, to kill water buffalo and adult **gaur** (GOWR), wild Asian cattle that weigh up to 2,200 pounds (1,000 kg). Depending upon where a tiger lives, its prey can be antelopes, wild goats, goat antelopes, wild cattle, bears, a kind of wild dog called **dholes** (DOHLZ), leopards, **tapirs,** wild boars, porcupines, and baby rhinos and elephants. Tiger prey also includes a wide variety of deer, such as moose, elk, sika deer, roe deer, hog deer, and **sambar.** A tiger's most common prey is medium-sized deer or antelope and wild boar.

The stripes of this hunting Bengal tiger help make it almost disappear when it hides in the grass.

Left top: *The main food of tigers includes a number of kinds of deer, like this spotted deer in India.*
Left bottom: *Tigers will also hunt animals as large as these water buffalo.*
Below: *A tiger may hunt by ambush, waiting hidden for prey to pass by.*

Scientists believe the average male tiger kills 65 to 75 **ungulates** (UHNG-yoo-lehts), or hoofed animals, yearly. The total weight of these animals is nearly 8,000 pounds (3,600 kg). A female tiger without cubs kills 45 to 50 ungulates, and one with cubs kills an average of 60 to 70.

A tiger's **stalk** may take minutes or more than an hour. When the tiger is within 100 feet (30 m) or so of its prey, it makes a sudden rush, usually attacking its victim from the rear. In open country, where hiding places are hard to find, a tiger may begin its charge from more than 300 feet (90 m) away. Far more often than not, the would-be victim of a tiger attack sees the tiger and escapes.

A tiger's size and strength knocks smaller prey off their feet like a ball hitting bowling pins. Larger prey may stay upright until the tiger's weight and strong, raking forepaws wrestle it to the ground. The tiger's agility, or quickness, helps it to attack and avoid the prey's thrashing horns, hooves, and in the case of wild boars, **tusks.**

Tigers kill animals of about 110 pounds (50 kg) or smaller with a bite through the neck or skull. A tiger usually kills larger animals by gripping the victim's throat in its jaws. Occasionally a tiger clamps its jaws onto the animal's nose. Either way, the animal dies from the lack of oxygen.

A tiger usually drags its fresh kill to a hiding place. These cats are so strong that they have been known to haul a kill nearly 400 yards (365 m)—the length of four football fields. The story is told of a tiger that dragged an enormous gaur almost 40 feet (12 m) into hiding. Thirteen men later tried to move the gaur. They couldn't budge it.

A tiger can gobble down 45 to 80 pounds (20–36 kg) of meat in a meal. It covers the leftovers with sticks and leaves. During the next several days, the tiger returns for meals, until the meat is gone or becomes too rotten even for the tiger's taste.

Above left: *A tiger may charge through water in an attack on prey.*
Above: *After a successful hunt, a tiger drags its buffalo kill to a hiding place to eat it.*

A tiger will return to the hiding place for several days to finish the meat.

A well-fed, contented tiger will lie on its back, as if it's inviting someone to scratch its white belly. But it wouldn't be so much an invitation as it would be a dare. A tiger is more than big enough to kill a human. Sometimes, tigers do kill humans.

Tigers hunt for survival, not sport—the easier the prey, the smaller the risk. Lacking tusks, horns, hooves—and sometimes good sense—unarmed people are easy prey. A very few tigers have apparently learned that and have sought out human prey, rather than just waiting for dumb luck to send the occasional human along. In most cases where tigers have attacked humans, the tigers were either defending their cubs or had been injured. Unable to chase fast four-legged prey, injured tigers may adapt to catching humans. Other tigers known to have killed people were young and had not learned that people, if they are carrying firearms, can be very dangerous.

Tigers, of course, are always armed with fangs and claws, and like any large **predator,** they are always a potential danger. When Singapore and nearby islands were being settled in the early 1800s, tigers killed several hundred people there each year. Around the same time, human-eating tigers made certain parts of India too dangerous for people. Even in the early 1900s, Bengal tigers may have killed as many as 1,000 people per year, although some tiger experts think that figure is too high.

A tigress in the Kumaon area of India reportedly killed 236 people between 1907 and 1911. If that's true, she rarely killed any prey except human beings. In 1922, tigers nearly turned a Chinese village into a ghost town in one week by killing 60 people.

Through the early 2000s, tigers have killed about 25 people each year in the Sundarbans, the swampy border region between Bangladesh and India. Since tigers usually attack from behind, Sundarbans villagers have begun wearing masks of human faces on the backs of their heads in an effort to discourage tigers from attacking them.

Curiously, tigers in other parts of tiger country, such as Russia and Indonesia, have never been linked to large numbers of human deaths. Still, over recorded time, tigers have killed more people than any other mammal has. That should not be surprising. After all, this largest of cats is one of nature's most perfect predators.

Sundarbans villagers wear masks on the back of their heads to protect them from tiger attacks.

Huge, powerful tigers begin as small tiger cubs.

BECOMING A TIGER

Before a tiger becomes a mighty cat with its fearsome stare and strong, supple body, it is a furry, blind, 3-pound (1.4-kg) cub. At birth and for several months afterward, it will depend upon its mother for food, protection, and instruction. A male tiger has no role in raising his cubs.

A mother tiger may give birth to as many as seven cubs at a time, but she usually has three or four. The cubs are born in a hidden area—a rock crevice, a space under a fallen log, or a tangle of branches and leaves. For two months, the cubs only drink their mother's milk.

The tigress can't always stay with her cubs because she has to hunt. When the cubs are ready for something besides milk but still too small to follow her, she brings food back to them by first eating it. Then she **regurgitates** (throws up) the food at the hideout. It is soft and pasty, perfect for young cubs.

A mother tiger instinctively keeps her cubs hidden. Dholes, leopards, bears, wolves, and even other tigers will kill tiger cubs. Flood, fire, and people are also threats. If a tigress senses danger, she will carry the cubs in her mouth, one at a time, to a new hideout. But despite a mother tiger's efforts, about one in every three tiger cubs dies within its first year from birth defects, from disease, or from having been killed by other animals.

When it is necessary, a mother tiger will defend her cubs fiercely. A tigress in Nepal severely clawed a research scientist who had come too close to her cubs. A tigress in India attacked and killed a male tiger that threatened her cubs. A father tiger isn't likely to kill his own cubs, if he happens to come into contact with them. But any other adult male is a real danger to them. The killing of cubs by an unrelated male tiger is a common event. Scientists think that a male tiger may kill cubs unrelated to him to improve the chances that his own cubs will survive.

When the cubs are very young, the mother tiger will hide them when she goes off to hunt.

The mother tiger is not only the cubs' protector. She is their teacher too. Whatever young tigers learn, they learn from her. At about 2 months of age, the cubs are old enough to begin to follow their mother when she hunts. Some scientists believe that the white spot behind each of a tiger's ears helps tiger cubs keep their mother in view. Though they are still too young to hunt themselves, they are old enough to begin feeding on their mother's kills. As the cubs grow and travel more easily, the tigress increases the size of her hunting range. In these early months, the cubs are beginning to learn how to hunt and kill.

Older cubs follow their mother to learn how to hunt and kill their own prey.

This Indochinese cub knows to stay close to its mother.

Young tigers learn patience and the finer points of hunting from their mother, but tigers are born with the instinct to stalk and kill. Like pet kittens, tiger cubs play-fight, stalk, charge, and pounce on each other. What seems like playful behavior sharpens the youngsters' hunting instincts and helps prepare them for adult life.

By 18 months, young tigers have permanent teeth. Although they have not reached full adult size, their long, sharp canine teeth—their killing teeth—are fully grown. The young tigers are able to begin killing large prey, at first with their mother's help. Later, they begin to hunt by themselves.

Cubs wrestle, stalk, and pounce in play to prepare for hunting as adults.

During the next 6 months, the young tigers become increasingly independent. They stay within their mother's home range, but they wander within it. The youngsters often spend more time with each other than with their mother.

As her cubs near adulthood, the tigress seeks a mate. She is ready to begin a new family. A new family leaves no room for the old one. The young tigers have already begun to drift away from their mother, and the tigress makes the split final. With a new family to care for, she drives her older cubs away.

No longer welcome on their mother's home range, young male tigers seek their own territories. It's a difficult and dangerous period for them. Each has grown up in his mother's home range, which was probably part of an adult male's territory. The resident adult male will rarely accept newly independent young males in his territory. The young males are forced to wander and generally settle for second- or third-best habitat with fewer prey animals.

The young tiger may try to force an adult male from its territory, resulting in a fight that the youngster is very likely to lose. Only when an older resident male tiger dies or becomes too old or injured to defend his territory is a younger male likely to take it over.

Young male tigers looking for a range of their own also fight with other young tigers. The injuries caused by these battles frequently lead to the death of one or both of the fighters.

Young adult males sometimes fight one another over hunting territories.

An adult male (like this Bengal) will attack any young male who invades his home range.

If he can survive or avoid fighting during this time of new independence, a hungry, young male tiger still faces danger. He may have to leave the relative safety of the jungle or forest in his search for food. Then he may wander into unfamiliar places, such as farms or villages. If he kills domestic animals, he will probably find himself in a conflict with people.

Young female tigers often remain with their mothers for a few weeks longer than their brothers. But they, too, finally leave and strike out to find their own home ranges. Sometimes a tigress permits one of her female cubs to settle on part of her territory.

Young tigers begin their own families when they are somewhere between 2 and 3 years of age. Young males, however, rarely have an opportunity to be fathers at that age. A female tiger looking for a mate would almost always have an older, larger male nearby. He would likely attack any young tiger that attempted to mate with the tigress.

Scientists are learning more about the habit of tigers, such as this Siberian.

TRACKING TIGERS

The number of wild tigers dropped alarmingly in the early 1970s. The World Wildlife Fund and the International Union of Concerned Naturalists (IUCN) convinced the governments of several nations where tigers live that the great cats were in danger of extinction. The governments of India and Nepal took the warning especially seriously and looked at ways to help tigers.

An important key to saving a wild animal species is to learn more about its life history. By doing so, researchers also learn more about what the species needs to survive. In 1973, scientists in Nepal began to trap tigers and attach **radio collars** to them. Using a tiny lithium battery, the radios beamed signals to researchers. By monitoring the signals, researchers learned about the tigers' travels and habits. Many more tigers in Nepal, India, Russia, and elsewhere were fitted with radio collars during the next 30 years.

In 1993, researchers added another research technique: camera trapping. Scientists rigged cameras to be set off by movement. They were placed along certain jungle trails. The different animals moving along the trails had their pictures taken when they tripped the camera's shutter. Sometimes that animal was a tiger, which gave researchers a bit more information about tigers' travels and ranges.

Above: *Tigers have been tracked with radio collars similar to this one.*
Right: *This tiger took his own photo when he set off a specially rigged camera.*

More recently, scientists have begun to use tiger radio collars with Global Positioning Systems (GPS). These high-tech collars beam signals to satellites that determine the animal's exact position on Earth. The information is directed back to the collar, where it is stored and later can be read electronically by researchers.

Despite high-tech methods, studying tigers is difficult. A tiger first has to be cornered and drugged so that it can be collared. Trucks, men on elephants and on foot, and even helicopters have been used to help capture tigers in order to attach radios. The efforts have helped scientists unlock many secrets of this secretive cat.

A worker riding an elephant sets out to track a tiger.

SAVING THE PERFECT PREDATOR

In some parts of Asia, people have worshiped tigers. They have made tigers favorite subjects of art, religion, and myth. Yet at the same time, tigers have been destroyed because they can be dangerous and are feared. China pushed for the complete elimination of tigers in the 1960s and came dangerously close to succeeding.

Facing page: *Tiger hunts were a popular sport until late in the twentieth century. This painting shows a tiger fighting back during a seventeenth-century hunt.*

Tigers have also been hunted because their gorgeous striped skins make exotic coats, rugs, and wall hangings. For most of the century past, we treated tigers as though they were more valuable dead than alive. One historian estimates that between 1875 and 1925, 80,000 tigers were killed in India alone. And as late as the 1960s, India and Nepal sold tiger hunts to wealthy sportsmen.

By the 1980s and 1990s, as tiger countries outlawed tiger hunting, **poachers** (people who hunt illegally) became increasingly active. Poachers killed not only tigers. They also killed tiger prey. A fair amount of tiger habitat in Asia doesn't have tigers because the ungulates that are food for tigers have been killed off by humans.

Tiger skins have been used for wall hangings, as well as for coats and rugs.

Poachers still destroy tigers, often for their body parts. People who practice traditional Chinese medicine have ground up the body parts of tigers and certain other wild animals for centuries. These people believe the body parts will cure various illnesses. Nearly one-quarter of the world's population is treated with traditional Chinese medicine, so the demand for tiger "medicine" is always present.

Humans have pushed wild tigers to the brink of extinction, but they aren't quite over the edge yet. Scientists continue to study tigers in the twenty-first century, but even by the 1980s, scientists had learned enough to know how wild tigers could be saved.

Tigers were also captured to appear in circuses and wild animal shows.

India created reserves to save its tigers, such as this Bengal cooling off in a river.

Convinced that tigers faced extinction in their countries, India and Nepal created new tiger reserves. These countries closed roads and hired police patrols to guard the new parks. They even moved entire villages out of reserves. Russia banned the hunting of tigers and enforced the law. The Siberian tiger population grew.

But with law enforcement lagging in the early 1990s, poachers in India killed large numbers of tigers for the illegal trade in tiger parts for medicine, largely in Taiwan, Japan, and China. Poachers struck in Russia too, where a new government did not have the money to police its tiger reserves. By 1994, the tiger population in Russia had dwindled to perhaps 250.

Meanwhile, in southern China, Cambodia, Laos, and Myanmar, the lush forests only looked like good tiger habitat. The animals that tigers hunt for food had been killed by local people.

Tiger conservation is a difficult task. Organizations that work to protect tigers often have to deal with government red tape. In exchange for money, some government officials are willing to ignore illegal activities, such as logging in tiger reserves. And the nations with wild tigers are not always as eager to save them as scientists are. Would you really want tigers in your backyard?

Most of the Asian countries with tigers are poor. Many face the possibility of war at almost any time. Nearly all of them have large, growing human populations. Many village people in or near tiger country are just trying to eke out a living. In their cultures, wildlife is often viewed as food, medicine, or a life-threatening danger. Tigers who kill villager's livestock make the lives of these people even more difficult.

Tigers at the Wuhan Animal Refuge in China capture their own food.

Captive tigers are fed at a reserve in Thailand.

One prospect for conserving tigers is the use of captive breeding sites sponsored by conservation organizations and governments. These sites safely house and feed captured wild animals and their offspring. Captive breeding sites could serve as a resource if tigers—or some other endangered animal—were about to disappear entirely from the wild.

Captive breeding programs, however, are expensive. The money spent maintaining them and their staffs does not really help tigers living in the wild. Most conservationists would prefer that money be spent on buying more land for tiger reserves or paying for more law enforcement on the reserves already established.

Other questions remain about where to best spend money and human effort. What is the greatest threat to wild tigers—being hunted for medicines or losing land and prey? Are any human activities, such as logging and farming, acceptable in tiger reserves? Are there even any tigers left to save in some areas? For instance, no one is sure that there are any South China tigers left in the wild.

Siberian tigers face an uncertain future in Russia and China.

These Sumatran tiger cubs will thrive if they are provided with habitat, prey, and protection.

Beyond these questions is a larger issue: Can Asian governments quickly be persuaded to provide the proper habitat, prey, and protection that tigers need? Tigers multiply quite easily if these three needs are satisfied.

Some people believe the tiger is doomed. But if humans have the will and resources to provide habitat, prey, and protection, the tiger may yet survive in the wild. Then the tiger's roar will still thunder for future generations in the snowy evergreen forests of Russia and in the misty forests of Southeast Asia.

GLOSSARY

adaptations: changes in a kind of living thing that help it survive certain living conditions

ambush: to lie in wait to attack

canine teeth: pointed teeth used for tearing flesh

carnivore: a meat eater

cub: a young tiger

dhole: a kind of wild dog

extinct: gone forever

fangs: pointed teeth; canine teeth

gaur: a kind of wild cattle

habitat: the place where a plant or animal usually lives

home range: the territory that a tiger protects as its hunting area

limber: agile or flexible

muzzle: the jaws and nose of an animal; snout

Panthera: the group of roaring cats

poachers: people who hunt animals illegally

predator: an animal that hunts

prey: an animal that is food for a hunting animal

prides: groups of lions

radio collars: small radios attached to collars. When placed on the necks of animals, these radios enable scientists to track the animals' movements.

regurgitates: throws up food

retract: to pull claws back into the paws

sambar: a large deer that lives in India and other parts of Asia

scent gland: a body organ that produces odors

stalk: the act of moving up on prey quietly

subspecies: groups of a specific animal that look slightly different and live in different areas

tapir: a piglike animal that lives in Indonesia and other places

tigress: a female tiger

tusks: long teeth that stick out of an animal's mouth

ungulates: animals with hooves

INDEX

ABOUT THE AUTHOR

Lynn M. Stone is an author and wildlife photographer who has written more than 400 books for young readers about wildlife and natural history. Mr. Stone enjoys fishing and travel and, of course, photographing wildlife. He is a former teacher and lives with his family in St. Charles, Illinois.

PHOTO ACKNOWLEDGEMENTS

Additional photographs courtesy of: © Erwin & Peggy Bauer, pp. 23 (upper and lower left), 24 (both); © Dinodia Photo Library, p. 26; © Royalty-free/CORBIS, p. 12; © Layne Kennedy/CORBIS, p. 36 (top); © Jim Kern Expeditions, pp. 36 (bottom), 37; © Francis G. Mayer/CORBIS, p. 38; © Robert Holmes/CORBIS, p. 39; © Swim Ink/CORBIS, p. 40; © Reuters/CORBIS, p. 42; © Martin Harvey; Gallo Images/CORBIS, p. 43; © Kevin Schafer, p. 45.

Front cover: © Lynn M. Stone